THE ULTIMATE
RETIREMENT
BUCKET LIST

THE ULTIMATE
RETIREMENT
BUCKET LIST

101 **FUN** THINGS TO DO, **EXCITING** EVERYDAY ACTIVITIES, AND **ONCE-IN-A-LIFETIME** EXPERIENCES FOR A HEALTHIER, **HAPPIER** THIRD ACT!

SARAH BILLINGTON

ULYSSES PRESS

Published in the United States by:
ULYSSES PRESS
P.O. Box 3440
Berkeley, CA 94703
www.ulyssespress.com

ISBN: 978-1-64604-003-2
Library of Congress Control Number: 2019951336

Printed in the United States by Kingery Printing Company
10 9 8 7 6 5 4 3 2 1

Acquisitions editor: Casie Vogel
Managing editor: Claire Chun
Editor: Renee Rutledge
Proofreader: Kathy Kaiser
Cover design: Justin Shirley
Cover art from shutterstock.com: disco ball © Vladvm; dogs © Nadya_Art; bicycle © Dark Ink; sailboat © SofiaV; palette © derter
Interior design: Jake Flaherty
Interior art from shutterstock.com: page 15 © N.Savranska; page 19 © thenatchdl; page 61 © KittyVector; page 62 GoodStudio; page 64 © GoodStudio; page 74 © Sabelskaya; pages 83, 84 © Badim36; page 85 © delcarmat; page 95 © singpentinkhappy; page 96 © Luciano Cosmo; page 101 © ivector; page 104 © ne2pi; page 105 © Dmitriy Samorodinov; page 107 © legdrubma; page 109 © robuart; page 110 © SunshineVector; page 111 © Sabelskaya; page 112 © Fagreia; page 113 © AkimD; page 114 © Aleutie; page 115 © Tartila

To my favorite retirees, who demonstrate daily how to live this stage of life and live it well: my parents, Colin and Hazell Billington.

CONTENTS

CHAPTER 7
Religion and Spirituality .63

CHAPTER 8
Creating Purpose 67

CHAPTER 9
Laugh Like You Mean It .73

CHAPTER 10
Creativity and Hobbies 81

CHAPTER 11
Education 87

CHAPTER 12
Living Dangerously 93

CHAPTER 13
Big Daring Dreams 99

CHAPTER 14
Seasonal Bucket Lists 103

Conclusion 117

Appendix 119

Acknowledgments 131

About the Author 132

INTRODUCTION

Congratulations, you did it! You made it through the trials and learning stages of childhood and early adulthood. You have worked hard and made a difference for your family, workplace, and community. Now it is time to enjoy the spoils of a long life and spend the coming years doing what you want to do. But what exactly do you want to do? It can be overwhelming to think about, so this book of 101 bucket list ideas is here to inspire you, help you narrow down what you want and don't want out of life, and get you excited about living the retirement that will bring you joy and help you thrive.

I have broken down the bucket lists into categories to accommodate a well-rounded lifestyle, combining specific suggestions with space to create your own, personal lists.

Working through a bucket list can make you stop for a moment and think about what you actually want to experience in this lifetime. What is important to you? What do you wish to accomplish? What are you curious about? These lists can remind you that life is short, and you should live it to the fullest.

By coming up with activities that align with your passions and interests, you are more likely to think outside the box and create a system that will help you break away from the routine that dominated your working life and old habits that no longer serve you. Writing down what you enjoy, what you don't enjoy, and your goals for the coming years will help you to commit to them as you gain clarity on what is important to you.

HOW TO USE THIS BOOK

This book will encourage you to reflect on your life, your skills, what you love doing and hate doing, and create a bucket list personal to you and deeply focused on enriching your life, fulfilling your deepest wishes, and creating a rewarding lifestyle you love.

Themed Bucket Lists

The themed categories in this book include expanding your social circle, investigating religion and spirituality, and daring to live dangerously. With each, you'll be guided through a variety of bucket list ideas, from exercise ideas to family-time plans, pushing you a little—or a lot—out of your comfort zone. People often call retirement the "third act," so why not make your third act the best it can possibly be? As you move through the ideas in this book, take the time to consider what feels right for you. After all, you are a one-of-a-kind human being and your retirement plans should be too.

Add Your Own Entries and Go at Your Own Pace

Whether you choose to spend a year on creativity, another on playfulness, and another on travel, whether you go it alone or check off your list with others, how you work your way through *The Ultimate Retirement Bucket List* is entirely up to you! The only rule is that you have fun doing it.

CHAPTER 1
BEFORE YOU BEGIN

Retirement is an exciting time to pursue anything that interests you (and avoid things that don't), but in order to experience the best of this time you need to acknowledge one important thing: You're getting older.

Don't let it hold you back. Age is just a number if you take care of your body and mind. Some of these bucket list ideas reflect new scientific findings on Alzheimer's disease and dementia prevention. Though these conditions are scary and unpredictable, you can add several activities to your daily routine to hold the symptoms at bay and live a long, happy life. Most of these lifestyle changes are as simple as socializing, exercising, or doing a crossword puzzle!

Research has found that simply walking for 45 minutes three times a week can increase brain volume (specifically of the hippocampus, the part of the brain in charge of memory) in those who are 65 years and older, and moving in the course of simple, everyday activities such as housework and cooking may make a difference in brain health in your 70s and 80s. So, as convenient as it is to order food services, hire a cleaner, or let loved ones take care of your errands in your twilight years, it's actually good for your brain health to hold onto these household chores.

BUCKET LIST BUDDIES

A whopping 101 ideas of things to do and lots of room to come up with more of your own is huge! Maybe a little overwhelming?

In order to achieve your goal of living your best life in retirement, without sleeping the days away or lazing about on the couch for weeks on end (unless that's on your list!), here's an idea to keep you on track: Make conquering your exciting but sometimes nerve-racking bucket list items more achievable and even more fun by recruiting a bucket list buddy!

Chances are, other people in your life would love to do some of the activities on your bucket list. So why not do them together? It will be more fun to bond and share memories of achieving your goals and checking them off your list together. In addition, when you schedule an activity with someone else, it makes you accountable so you're more likely to go through with it. And if you put it off, then you won't be disappointing just yourself but your loved one who wants to experience it too.

Does your son want to go to the ball game? Would your partner enjoy a wine and paint date night with you? Would a best friend want to take a cupcake-decorating class or hike a mountain to marvel at the views?

Your bucket list buddy need not be only one person. One loved one may be interested in doing several of the items on your list, and another may be excited about several others.

If you are sharing *The Ultimate Retirement Bucket List* journey with someone else, maybe they have chosen activities for their list that you hadn't thought of. You could be their bucket list buddy and try some new experiences you hadn't thought of as well.

Use parts of your bucket list as a way to spend more time enjoying activities and adventures with the people you love.

SMART GOAL SETTING

Knowing what you want to do is one thing, but sometimes that's not enough. There is a practically foolproof method for setting goals and following through with them and it's incredibly SMART.

First, organize your ideas into different groups, such as relationships, career, physical health, emotional health, living, finances, creativity, travel, religion/spirituality, education, fun and leisure, etc. Feel free to use the categories in this book as a guide.

Next, give yourself a clear time frame for achieving your goals. If your goal is short-term (for example, in three months, when you visit a specific city), long-term (such as a New Year's resolution, within the next year, in five years, etc.), or for a special occasion (for an anniversary or milestone), get a clear focus on what is most important to you.

Once your goals are broken down into rough time frames, see if you can narrow them down even more. What can you work toward achieving in the next month or week?

Remember that bigger goals, such as learning a language, might take a while to reach and you will have to take many steps to get there. Breaking up a big goal into smaller goals can help you achieve it sooner.

As the saying goes, "goals without plans are just dreams." If you haven't used the SMART goal-setting technique before or it's been a while, here's how to create and start checking off those bucket list items and living the retirement of your dreams with a little planning. SMART goals need to be:

- **S**pecific

- **M**easurable

- **A**ttainable

- **R**ealistic and Relevant

- **T**ime-limited and Trackable

Here's an example goal for getting SMART: I want to read more books.

Specific

If you've always enjoyed reading but weren't able to find the time for it while working and running a household, reading more is a great goal! But "reading more" is too loose a goal to help you actually achieve something concrete. You need to get specific.

The more specific you get, the more likely you will be to follow through.

Think about what types of books you want to read. When do you like reading best? Before you go to sleep, or while you're eating a meal? Where do you like to read? Do you want to read an hour before bed, tucked up under the blankets? At lunchtime, while you eat? Or maybe you want to listen to audio-books when you go for a daily walk. Do you prefer hardback books, ebooks, or paperbacks? How will you access books to read? Do you have shelves full of unread books, will you buy them in a store or online, or will you check them out from the library? Do you want to share the reading experience with a friend or loved one? You may want to join or form a book club to discuss and analyze what you read.

Why do you want to read more books? Do you actually want to read graphic novels because you enjoy the art form? Do you actually want to read more nonfiction and learn new things, or perhaps get back into a hobby you have previously enjoyed? With each goal you set and add to your bucket list, get specific about why it's important to you and how you will achieve it.

Choose some specific books you are excited about reading (and start your list on page 14!).

Measurable

Goals need to be measurable. Otherwise, how will you know whether you completed them or not? "I want to read more books" is not measurable. "I want to read a book every month," or "I want to read for half an hour every day this year" is.

Attainable

In this step, determine whether your goal of, say, reading a book a month is an attainable one for you. Can you afford to buy a new book every month? Do you have access to bookstores or libraries in your area? Does your life-style have room for 4 to 10 hours of reading each month? Do you have a quiet place or quiet time in your day to spend with a good book? Here, you can determine whether your goal needs some adjusting.

Realistic and Relevant

Realistic. Deciding that you want to read a book a week for the next year is a lofty goal, and depending on your lifestyle, your reading speed, and the length of the books you plan to read, it is likely to be a bit unrealistic for many. Aiming high is wonderful, but if your goal is unrealistic and destined to fail, it can impact your belief in your ability to achieve other goals too. If some of your goals are too ambitious or unrealistic for your lifestyle—and the other bucket list items on your agenda right now—step it back to something that will be easier to achieve. You can make your goals more challenging as you go.

Relevant. It's important to have realistic goals, but, more important, make sure that the goal is relevant to you. Why do you want to do it? If committing to reading, say, a book of classic fiction a month is going to be a chore because you don't actually enjoy classics, is it a goal you really want to commit to? Maybe it's a goal you feel you should want, just to say you achieved it. But if you find classics boring this isn't a relevant goal for you. This bucket list is about you and what you want out of your retirement. Pick up the police procedurals, rural romances, celebrity biographies, car magazines, or whatever is relevant to you instead!

Time-Limited and Trackable

If you don't give yourself a deadline, are you likely to finish your goal? Think about it. Without a date to complete challenging tasks that make you step outside your comfort zone or require a lot of time, commitment, or money, how likely are you to do it? Will you put it off? Are you likely to tell yourself you'll do it tomorrow or next week or next year, but tomorrow, next week, and next year never come? We've all been through this.

This book is full of activities and challenges that you want to do, so why put them off? Give yourself a deadline that is reasonable but also pushes you a little, then track your progress.

If you want to read a book a month, that gives you a time limit. You have one month—and it's trackable: When you hit "the end" of a book each month you have evidence that you have completed it.

You now have a SMART road map to work your way through your bucket list and keep track of your amazing progress.

IMPORTANT QUESTIONS ABOUT YOU

Before getting fired up and adding ideas to your bucket lists all willy-nilly, take a step back and reflect on your life to really understand what you have enjoyed in the past, what you have not enjoyed, existing skills you'd like to make use of, and skills you'd like to develop. Let what you discover about yourself inform what you could enjoy in the future.

Just because you think you should be doing more of something now that you're retired doesn't mean that it's right for you. The cliché of retirement depicts days on the golf course, lawn bowling, or sewing quilts. If this sounds like heaven to you, fantastic! But if not, then don't even think about those activities again.

Have a good brainstorm about the following eight questions:

1. *What am I passionate about?*

Are you head over heels in love with your grandkids? Have you always enjoyed woodworking, but it's been years since you picked up the tools? Are you obsessed with ice skating, watching motorsports, or maybe making pasta from scratch? What are some interests that you've always had but never fully explored? List the top five things you're most passionate about below:

1. _____

2. _____

3. _____

4. _____

5. _____

2. What am I skilled at and what do I enjoy doing now?

You have spent a lifetime cultivating skills that you may not even consider skills. Are you an excellent public speaker? Can you disarm a toddler before they explode into a tantrum? Do animals flock to you and obey your every word? Do you make new friends easily and put people at ease? Are you the funniest person in any room you enter? Maybe you're fantastic with money or have an amazing general knowledge of history. Think back on your life and feel good about all the things you've achieved and the skills you've taken the time to learn—on purpose or by happenstance. Thinking about these things helps boost self-esteem and joy. Who knows, perhaps you can put this lifetime of skills to good use for a volunteer cause. List three skills that you've cultivated throughout the years:

1. _____

2. _____

3. _____

3. What am I not currently skilled at, what do I dislike doing now?

As important as it is to reflect on what you're good at and enjoy, it's just as important to acknowledge what you dislike doing or what, no matter how hard you try, you simply haven't been able to master. For example, if you loathe washing dishes, investing in a dishwasher could make your days happier. Or, perhaps, you never want to give a speech again. While some people come alive when speaking in front of a crowd or leading a group in a project, you may loathe it every time or experience overwhelming anxiety, even if you are an amazing public speaker. And that's perfectly okay! If it's something you dislike doing, no matter how good you are at it, you might enjoy some relief by deliberately putting your public speaking days behind you. Write down those activities you want to let go from your life to give you clarity moving forward.

Note: Gaining some clarity on activities to move on from during this next phase of your life doesn't mean getting selfish with your time or neglecting those who need you!

_____

_____

_____

_____

_____

_____

_____

4. Of all the things I could spend my time doing, how do I want to spend my retirement years? How do I see myself spending my time?

_____

_____

_____

_____

_____

_____

_____

5. *Of my current lifestyle and life commitments, which do I want to do less of or stop participating in entirely?*

_____

_____

_____

_____

_____

_____

_____

6. *Which of my current life commitments do I enjoy, want to embrace, and do more of in my retirement?*

_____

_____

_____

_____

_____

_____

_____

7. *Current life commitments I want to scale back or move on from:*

_____

_____

_____

_____

_____

_____

_____

8. *What does an ideal day in retirement look like?*

_____

_____

_____

_____

_____

_____

_____

CHAPTER 2
FUN AND LEISURE

Let's start with some easy, fun ideas that I bet you've already thought about in the lead-up to your well-earned extended vacation.

1. BOOKS TO READ ❏

Have you always meant to read the classics, like *To Kill a Mockingbird* or *The Iliad*? How about everything ever by an author, like Nora Roberts or Michael Connelly? Did you love DC comics as a kid, or would you like to give poetry or memoirs a try? Create a list of the top 20 books you'd like to read. If you need some help, browse The *New York Times* Best Sellers list or the Pulitzer Prize website, which lists all the winners going back to 1917!

❏ 1. _____

❏ 2. _____

❏ 3. _____

❏ 4. _____

❏ 5. _____

❏ 6. _____

❏ 7. _____

❏ 8. _____

❏ 9. _____

❏ 10. _____

❏ 11. _____

❏ 12. _____

❏ 13. _____

❏ 14. _____

❏ 15. _____

❏ 16. _____

❑ 17. _____

❑ 18. _____

❑ 19. _____

❑ 20. _____

2₀ MOVIES TO SEE ❑

Have you been meaning to watch The Godfather trilogy? How about Rodgers and Hammerstein musicals, Alfred Hitchcock films, or Michael Bay's collected works? Write your list here.

❑ _____

❑ _____

❑ _____

❑ _____

❑ _____

❑ _____

❑ _____

❑ _____

❑ _____

❑ _____

❑ _____

❑ _____

❑ _____

❑ _____

❑ _____

❑ _____

❑ _____

3. TV SHOWS TO BINGE-WATCH ❏

What are some shows that you loved from your youth and have been meaning to see again? Are there some you've been wanting to watch but never got around to? Ask your friends and family for film and TV recommendations. You'll get to know what they enjoy and have some great, in-depth conversations ahead of you! List the TV shows to watch here.

❏ _____

❏ _____

❏ _____

❏ _____

❏ _____

❏ _____

❏ _____

❏ _____

❏ _____

❏ _____

❏ _____

❏ _____

❏ _____

❏ _____

❏ _____

❏ _____

4. ACADEMY AWARD BEST PICTURE– NOMINATED FILMS TO WATCH THIS YEAR ❑

Why spend your life watching bad movies? Commit to watching the best of the best and see all of the year's critically acclaimed, award-nominated films, starting with the Oscars. List the year's best-picture nominated films here.

❑ _____

❑ _____

❑ _____

❑ _____

❑ _____

❑ _____

❑ _____

❑ _____

❑ _____

❑ _____

❑ _____

❑ _____

5. TWELVE FILMS IN TWELVE DIFFERENT LANGUAGES IN ONE YEAR

Foreign films are not only populated with characters speaking in a different language from your own, but they expose you to different cultures and ways of life as well. List the films you plan to watch and what language they're in.

❑ 1. _____

❑ 2. _____

❑ 3. _____

❑ 4. _____

❑ 5. _____

❑ 6. _____

❑ 7. _____

❑ 8. _____

❑ 9. _____

❑ 10. _____

❑ 11. _____

❑ 12. _____

6. RECIPES TO COOK ❑

List recipes that have defeated you in the past, or perhaps from cuisines you've never tried before that excite you.

❑ _____

❑ _____

❑ _____

❑ _____

❑ _____

❑ _____

❑ _____

❑ _____

❑ _____

❑ _____

❑ _____

❑ _____

❑ _____

❑ _____

❑ _____

❑ _____

❑ _____

❑ _____

7. NEW PURSUITS TO TRY

❑

Trampolining? Screen printing? Agility training with your dog? Write your list here.

❑ _____

❑ _____

❑ _____

❑ _____

❑ _____

❑ _____

❑ _____

❑ _____

❑ _____

❑ _____

❑ _____

❑ _____

❑ _____

❑ _____

❑ _____

❑ _____

❑ _____

CHAPTER 3
TRAVEL ADVENTURES NEAR AND FAR

Not every retirement budget can stretch to include summers in Australia and winters on the slopes of Aspen, but far-off destinations aren't the only places worthy of exploration. How many times have you taken local attractions in your city or day trip destinations for granted, telling yourself you'll go eventually, one day, when you have time? It's not uncommon for tourists to see more, do more, and know more about a destination than the locals do. So why wait any longer?

8. LOCAL ATTRACTIONS TO VISIT ❑

❑ _____

❑ _____

❑ _____

❑ _____

❑ _____

❑ _____

❑ _____

❑ _____

❑ _____

❑ _____

❑ _____

❑ _____

❑ _____

❑ _____

❑ _____

❑ _____

❑ _____

❑ _____

❑ _____

℘₀ RESTAURANTS TO DINE AT ❑

❑ _____

❑ _____

❑ _____

❑ _____

❑ _____

❑ _____

❑ _____

❑ _____

❑ _____

❑ _____

❑ _____

❑ _____

❑ _____

❑ _____

❑ _____

❑ _____

❑ _____

❑ _____

❑ _____

10. FESTIVALS/EVENTS TO ATTEND ❏

❏ _____

❏ _____

❏ _____

❏ _____

❏ _____

❏ _____

❏ _____

❏ _____

❏ _____

❏ _____

❏ _____

❏ _____

❏ _____

❏ _____

❏ _____

❏ _____

❏ _____

❏ _____

❏ _____

11. DAY TRIPS TO TAKE ❑

Organizing a day trip doesn't have to be a big chore, working out exactly where to go and how to get there. Why not book one that's already on offer? Join a winery tour, antiques tour, art museum tour, coastal road trip, or horseback riding tour. By joining a tour, all of the planning and organization has been done for you. All you need to do is get there on time and, potentially, make new friends with similar interests.

❑ _____

❑ _____

❑ _____

❑ _____

❑ _____

❑ _____

❑ _____

❑ _____

❑ _____

❑ _____

❑ _____

❑ _____

❑ _____

❑ _____

❑ _____

❑ _____

12. WEEKEND TRIPS TO TAKE ❑

A minibreak can be just as good as a vacation! What towns or cities within a couple of hours of you have you always wanted to visit? Who would be your perfect travel partner? Perhaps you'd like to visit some places solo.

❑ _____

❑ _____

❑ _____

❑ _____

❑ _____

❑ _____

❑ _____

❑ _____

❑ _____

❑ _____

❑ _____

❑ _____

❑ _____

❑ _____

❑ _____

❑ _____

❑ _____

13. INTERNATIONAL DESTINATIONS TO EXPERIENCE ❑

There are so many places to visit around the world, from deserts and pyramids in Egypt to the wilds of Africa or rolling green hills and quaint castles in Switzerland. Where do you want to go? And how do you want to travel? By cruise or train? Do you want to rent an RV, stay in a tiny house, or rent a houseboat? List your dream travel destinations and experiences here.

❑ _____

❑ _____

❑ _____

❑ _____

❑ _____

❑ _____

❑ _____

❑ _____

❑ _____

❑ _____

❑ _____

❑ _____

❑ _____

❑ _____

❑ _____

❑ _____

CHAPTER 4
COMMON DEATHBED REGRETS

Depending on when you retire, you'll probably have decades of time to fill! But it is still worth reflecting: If you were to die tomorrow, what do you wish you'd done differently in your life? It may feel morbid and a bit uncomfortable, but thinking about this now means you have the time to change it, find closure, rebuild relationships, right wrongs, and do the things you dreamed of when something in your life stopped you.

Did you lose touch with someone important to you? Did you always want to climb a mountain, write a novel, or ride a camel? Add them to your bucket list here.

14. RELATIONSHIPS TO REPAIR ❑

❑ _____

❑ _____

❑ _____

❑ _____

❑ _____

❑ _____

❑ _____

❑ _____

❑ _____

❑ _____

❑ _____

❑ _____

❑ _____

❑ _____

❑ _____

❑ _____

❑ _____

❑ _____

15. PEOPLE YOU'VE LOST TOUCH WITH TO CALL, TEXT, OR E-MAIL ❏

❏ _____

❏ _____

❏ _____

❏ _____

❏ _____

❏ _____

❏ _____

❏ _____

❏ _____

❏ _____

❏ _____

❏ _____

❏ _____

❏ _____

❏ _____

❏ _____

❏ _____

❏ _____

16. WHOM DO YOU OWE A VISIT THAT YOU'VE BEEN PUTTING OFF SEEING? ❑

❑ _____

❑ _____

❑ _____

❑ _____

❑ _____

❑ _____

❑ _____

❑ _____

❑ _____

❑ _____

❑ _____

❑ _____

❑ _____

❑ _____

❑ _____

❑ _____

❑ _____

17. SEND BIRTHDAY CARDS

It's hard to keep track of birthdays, but receiving a card in the mail is always such a pleasant surprise as it shows that someone truly cares for you. Make a list of friends' birthdays and set the goal of sending each of them a nice, personalized birthday note when the time comes.

❑ _____

❑ _____

❑ _____

❑ _____

❑ _____

❑ _____

❑ _____

❑ _____

❑ _____

❑ _____

❑ _____

❑ _____

❑ _____

❑ _____

❑ _____

❑ _____

❑ _____

18. LIVE YOUR LIFE TRUE TO YOURSELF, NOT WHAT OTHERS EXPECT OF YOU ❑

Many of us spend our lives the way we think we should, getting a well-paid but uninspiring job rather than following our passions that may not bring in as much money, or settling down with a mortgage to pay and feeling stuck in one place rather than visiting or living in other states or countries. What are your longest held, wildest dreams? Write them here and commit to pursuing at least three of them.

❑ _____

❑ _____

❑ _____

❑ _____

❑ _____

❑ _____

❑ _____

❑ _____

❑ _____

❑ _____

❑ _____

❑ _____

❑ _____

❑ _____

❑ _____

CHAPTER 5
RELATIONSHIPS: EXPAND YOUR SOCIAL CIRCLE

Just because you have a lot more spare time doesn't mean the people you enjoy spending time with do as well. Your children may still have jobs and have children of their own to care for, just as your friends may still be working and caring for their own families. Even your spouse or partner may not have retired yet, which could leave you feeling like you're rattling around the house alone, with nothing to do.

Don't risk becoming isolated in retirement. Here, you'll find tips on how to boost your social life to be as full and enriching as you want it to be. Go through your bucket lists with your bucket list buddies! Encourage loved ones to create bucket lists of their own and pick activities you can do together. Whether it's a one-off activity or a new skill or hobby that will take months or even years to learn, you can enjoy each other's company while feeling the reward of doing something that's important to you and checking that item off the list.

19. PEOPLE TO SPEND MORE TIME WITH ❑

Who has been a part of your life that you really enjoy but don't see as often as you'd like? List them here and, if they would also like to, make plans to reconnect.

❑ _____

❑ _____

❑ _____

❑ _____

❑ _____

❑ _____

❑ _____

❑ _____

❑ _____

❑ _____

❑ _____

❑ _____

❑ _____

❑ _____

❑ _____

❑ _____

❑ _____

20. PEOPLE TO SPEND LESS TIME WITH ❑

Some people move in and out of our lives over the years for various reasons, and some aren't meant to be a part of our lives forever. If there are people you find drain you or bring you down or take up too much of your time or emotional space, write their names down here. Silently thank them for the memories you shared together, wish them well, and mentally let them go to make room for those who fulfill you.

❑ _____

❑ _____

❑ _____

❑ _____

❑ _____

❑ _____

❑ _____

❑ _____

❑ _____

❑ _____

❑ _____

❑ _____

❑ _____

❑ _____

❑ _____

❑ _____

21. ACQUAINTANCES TO GET TO KNOW BETTER ❑

Is there someone you know peripherally but feel like you might really click with? Try to set up a coffee date or Sunday brunch with them to develop your friendship.

❑ _____

❑ _____

❑ _____

❑ _____

❑ _____

❑ _____

❑ _____

❑ _____

❑ _____

❑ _____

❑ _____

❑ _____

❑ _____

❑ _____

❑ _____

❑ _____

❑ _____

22. PLACES TO MEET YOUR COMMUNITY ❑

Every day you're out in public, strike up a conversation with a stranger. Everyone has an interesting story to share. List a few places in your community where you could have conversations with people you don't know.

❑ _____

❑ _____

❑ _____

❑ _____

❑ _____

❑ _____

❑ _____

❑ _____

❑ _____

❑ _____

❑ _____

❑ _____

❑ _____

❑ _____

❑ _____

❑ _____

❑ _____

23. SPECIAL HEIRLOOMS AND EXPENSIVE BELONGINGS TO USE ❑

Some items we own are too special or too expensive to risk damaging. But what's the point of owning them if you don't use them? List all the special items you own that you haven't used, but should!

❑ _____

❑ _____

❑ _____

❑ _____

❑ _____

❑ _____

❑ _____

❑ _____

❑ _____

❑ _____

❑ _____

❑ _____

❑ _____

❑ _____

❑ _____

❑ _____

❑ _____

24. TREASURED ITEMS TO PASS DOWN AND ENJOY WITH LOVED ONES ❑

Do you have a set of good china that never gets used because you're worried about breaking it? Do you have expensive jewelry or other items that stay in their drawer where no one can touch them? What's the point in owning precious items if no one gets to enjoy them? Pass them on to loved ones who will appreciate them. Take pleasure in their enjoyment in person, if possible.

❑ _____

❑ _____

❑ _____

❑ _____

❑ _____

❑ _____

❑ _____

❑ _____

❑ _____

❑ _____

❑ _____

❑ _____

❑ _____

❑ _____

❑ _____

25. PEOPLE TO BE VULNERABLE AND HAVE A CLOSER RELATIONSHIP WITH ❑

Being vulnerable and sharing secret insecurities and concerns with others can be hard. But letting people in allows them to support you and gives them the opportunity to share their own worries. Maybe you have the same problems or worries and can share tips on how you are handling them. Being vulnerable helps deepen connections and make relationships stronger. List people you would like to have a closer relationship with here.

❑ _____

❑ _____

❑ _____

❑ _____

❑ _____

❑ _____

❑ _____

❑ _____

❑ _____

❑ _____

❑ _____

❑ _____

❑ _____

❑ _____

❑ _____

26. ELDERLY LOVED ONES TO SPEND MORE TIME WITH

❑

Create a list of elderly people in your life you don't see as often as you could, and make an effort to visit and spend time with them. Help them with things around the house they find a bit harder these days, teach them how to use a new technology that will make their lives easier, pick up their groceries, or take their dog to the groomers. Talk with your loved ones and hear their stories. They won't be around forever, so take the opportunity while you have it, as you hope others will do for you in the decades to come.

❑ _____

❑ _____

❑ _____

❑ _____

❑ _____

❑ _____

❑ _____

❑ _____

❑ _____

❑ _____

❑ _____

❑ _____

❑ _____

❑ _____

❑ _____

CHAPTER 6
HEALTHY HABITS

Do you stay up too late watching TV and feel rotten the next day? Do you drink more alcohol than you would like to, drink less water than you should, or spend a lot of time at home alone, on the couch? Everyone at every stage of life has some habits that aren't helpful or healthy, and that they would feel better giving up or changing. There's nothing wrong with staying up late on its own, but if it means you consistently wake up feeling like a zombie, lethargic, like your brain is full of cotton candy, then it might be a habit to consider changing so that you can feel better.

Take it slow, you don't need to make life hard on yourself and go from hitting the hay at 3 a.m. to going to bed at 8 p.m. overnight. Start by bringing your bedtime forward by 15 minutes for a couple of nights, then 15 minutes more for a couple of nights until you start feeling sleepy at a reasonable hour and are refreshed and energetic in the morning.

27. HABITS TO CHANGE

WHAT I DO NOW	THE HABIT I WANT TO FORM	HOW I'M GOING TO SLOWLY CHANGE MY HABIT
Example: Go to bed at 3 a.m. and sleep the mornings away.	Example: Go to bed by 9 p.m. and feel alert and active during the day.	Example: Go to bed 15 minutes earlier every 3 days until I reach a 9 p.m. bedtime.

Tip: There will be setbacks—you're only human! Don't beat yourself up about it, simply get back on the wagon as soon as you can.

USE IT OR LOSE IT: PHYSICAL HEALTH

Let's be real. You may not be able to do all the things you could when you were younger, but just because you're slowing down a little doesn't mean you need to stop or give up entirely. In fact, studies have found an age-related deterioration of 1 to 2% per year in both muscle mass and strength in older adults,[1] but strength training as you age can delay this decline. To maintain independence as you age, it's important to stay active, for both your physical and mental health (find more on mental health on page 53). But that doesn't mean you need to pump iron if that's never been your thing. Find physical activities you enjoy and can commit to regularly, and reap not only the physical benefits but the mental (and potentially social) ones too!

TAKE MY VITAMINS AND MEDICATIONS EVERY DAY FOR 30 DAYS

We all need to take care of our bodies, providing them with the nutrients we need and the medications for those ailments that come with age. Start using a medication tracker for 30 days to form a solid habit. Before you fill out the tracker on page 120, photocopy it so that you can start again each month and keep track of whether you have taken or forgotten your medication each day. Though not the most exciting item on a bucket list, it will help you to start—or solidify—good habits.

---

1   Walter Frontera and Xavier Bigard, "The Benefits of Strength Training in the Elderly," *Science & Sports* 17 (2002): 109-116, doi: 10.1016/SO765-1597(02)00135-1.

28. MOVE MORE—PHYSICAL ACTIVITIES YOU HAVE ENJOYED IN THE PAST THAT YOU'D LIKE TO TRY AGAIN ❏

❏ _____

❏ _____

❏ _____

❏ _____

❏ _____

❏ _____

❏ _____

❏ _____

❏ _____

❏ _____

❏ _____

❏ _____

❏ _____

❏ _____

❏ _____

❏ _____

❏ _____

❏ _____

29. PHYSICAL ACTIVITIES YOU HAVE NEVER DONE BUT HAVE ALWAYS WANTED TO TRY ❏

❏ _____

❏ _____

❏ _____

❏ _____

❏ _____

❏ _____

❏ _____

❏ _____

❏ _____

❏ _____

❏ _____

❏ _____

❏ _____

❏ _____

❏ _____

❏ _____

❏ _____

❏ _____

30. TAKE A DANCE CLASS AND LEARN A ROUTINE ❏

If you used to dance and haven't done so in a while or you were always a wallflower and thought dancing wasn't your thing, now's the time to revisit this fun way to get moving. Studies have shown that due to the challenge of learning new moves, dancing even has an antiaging effect on the brain[2], so slip into your dancing shoes! There are so many different styles and dance techniques that you never know what you might enjoy! Try a beginners' class in hip-hop, ballroom, Latin, swing, or even Broadway-style dancing! You're not trying to go pro but find an active, social hobby that gets your heart pumping and makes you smile. You tried ballroom and didn't enjoy it? No problem, maybe hip-hop is more your style!

31. RESEARCH THE TEN HIGHEST PEAKS IN YOUR STATE AND CLIMB THREE OF THEM ❏

Take it slow and steady or, if you're in great shape, power up those peaks! Once you reach the top, marvel at amazing vistas and feel pride in your accomplishments. Depending on the difficulty of your hike, be sure to prepare appropriately with adequate supplies and equipment to get you up and back safely. List the peaks you plan to climb here.

❏ _____

❏ _____

❏ _____

---

2 *Frontiers.* "Dancing Can Reverse the Signs of Aging in the Brain." ScienceDaily. www.sciencedaily.com/releases/2017/08/170825124902.htm (accessed September 17, 2019).

MENTAL AND EMOTIONAL WELL-BEING

Your frame of mind and attitude can deeply affect your outlook on retirement. It's hard to adapt to a big lifestyle change like retirement, so it's important to set yourself up for success with a strong, positive state of mind. It's unfortunately all too common for new retirees to enjoy the freedom of retirement at first but begin to feel lost, lonely, bored, and without direction after a time. Feeling like you no longer have anything to contribute to society can make the years ahead look disappointing and frightening. Indeed, a study by the National Bureau of Economic Research found that retirement from the workforce can decrease mental health in individuals by 6 to 9% over the course of six years.[3]

Those who plan ahead and make a conscious effort to get out of the house and socialize, remain active, take part in the world around them, and create a goal for their retirement are happier and more fulfilled during these years. Finding gratitude for your past and excitement for the journey ahead will help you accept that the past is in the past and your future is bright. Even if you aren't necessarily happy when you think of your past, it's important to accept it so you don't move forward with regrets. Plus, now is the time you can change your future, and that's yet another thing to be grateful for!

3   Dhaval Dave, Inas Rashad, and Jasmina Spasojevic, "The Effects of Retirement on Physical and Mental Health Outcomes," *Southern Economic Journal* 75, no. 2 (2008): 497-523.

32. PAST WOUNDS TO HEAL ❑

What are some regrets that still trouble you periodically or even constantly? Now could be the time to address them, apologize to someone, or fix a wrong. The people you feel deserve an apology may have let it go a long time ago, and by talking to them about it or making it right you will find that you can let it go too.

But take note, just because you apologize does not mean they are obligated to forgive you.

❑ _____

❑ _____

❑ _____

❑ _____

❑ _____

❑ _____

❑ _____

❑ _____

❑ _____

❑ _____

❑ _____

❑ _____

❑ _____

❑ _____

❑ _____

33. LIVE IN THE NOW: PRACTICE MINDFULNESS ONCE A DAY FOR SEVEN DAYS IN A ROW ❑

When feeling stressed, anxious, depressed, or any other emotion you don't want to be feeling, mindfulness can help you recenter, and it can be done anywhere you choose as follows: Close your eyes and, taking slow, calming breaths, concentrate on three to five things, one at a time, that you can hear. Then three to five things you can smell, then feel, then taste. Open your eyes and look around you, then focus on three to five things you can see. When you are truly grounded in the moment like this, you will find you can't think about anything else.

❑ MONDAY _____

❑ TUESDAY _____

❑ WEDNESDAY _____

❑ THURSDAY _____

❑ FRIDAY _____

❑ SATURDAY _____

❑ SUNDAY _____

34. EXPAND YOUR COMFORT ZONE ❑

Once a day for a full month do something that slightly scares you. If you're shy, say hello to a stranger. Make your comfort zone larger, and you will feel more confident in a variety of ways and gain the confidence to try even more things that scare you.

❑ 1. _____

❑ 2. _____

❑ 3. _____

❑ 4. _____

❑ 5. _____

❑ 6. _____

❑ 7. _____

❑ 8. _____

❑ 9. _____

❑ 10. _____

❑ 11. _____

❑ 12. _____

❑ 13. _____

❑ 14. _____

❑ 15. _____

❑ 16. _____

❑ 17. _____

❑ 18. _____

❑ 19. _____

❑ 20. _____

❑ 21. _____

❑ 22. _____

❑ 23. _____

❑ 24. _____

❑ 25. _____

❑ 26. _____

❑ 27. _____

❑ 28. _____

❑ 29. _____

❑ 30. _____

❑ 31. _____

35. KEEP A MOOD DIARY FOR SEVEN DAYS

Track your mood every day for a week. Try to connect what happens each day with how you feel about it. What were you doing on the days you felt best? Do more of that!

MONDAY

TUESDAY

WEDNESDAY

THURSDAY

FRIDAY

SATURDAY

SUNDAY

36. SPEND A WEEK BEING GRATEFUL

We often notice the things that irritate us and that we don't like in our lives but pay little attention to the things that run smoothly or that bring us joy. Spend a week taking deliberate notice of all of the good things—big and small—that happen in your life. From a refreshing night's sleep, delicious coffee, and a pleasant environment to a fantastic night out, pride in exercising every day for a week even on the days you didn't want to, or undertaking an exhilarating bucket list experience. Take the time to stop and be grateful. Focusing on the good helps you see the good more often. Write down three things you are grateful for each day for a week.

I am grateful for...

MONDAY

1. _____

2. _____

3. _____

TUESDAY

1. _____

2. _____

3. _____

WEDNESDAY

1. _____

2. _____

3. _____

THURSDAY

1. _____

2. _____

3. _____

FRIDAY

1. _____

2. _____

3. _____

SATURDAY

1. _____

2. _____

3. _____

SUNDAY

1. _____

2. _____

3. _____

37. MEDITATE DAILY FOR TWO WEEKS

Sit or lie down somewhere comfortable and concentrate on your breathing for two minutes or more, breathing slowly, deeply in and deeply out again. If your mind wanders, that's fine. Just bring your thoughts back to your breath.

38. CARE FOR YOUR SKIN

Do something nice for the skin that you're in twice a week for a month. It could be getting a facial or doing a face mask at home, moisturizing your whole body if it's not something you regularly do, or giving yourself a manicure. Your skin is the largest organ of your body and it's important to give it attention.

39. WALK MORE ❑

Park farther away, take an extra flight of stairs, get off the bus a stop early, or even clean your home yourself; you've heard this one before but it's all true: Every little bit of movement counts!

40. TRAIN FOR AND RUN/WALK A 5K CHARITY RUN ❑

Show everyone—including yourself—that you may be retired but there's a lot of life left in you!

CHAPTER 7
RELIGION AND SPIRITUALITY

Feeling connected to something greater than yourself and those around you is important in every stage of life, especially when transitioning through a large lifestyle change like retiring. If your personal relationship with a higher power has lapsed, now is a great time to reconnect. If you're not religious or spiritual, researching different belief systems can help you understand others and their values.

41. START A PRAYER JOURNAL ❑

Whether speaking to God or sending prayers into the universe.

42. PRACTICE QUIET CONTEMPLATION ❑

Life is so busy, our minds so cluttered in the age of 24/7 news cycles that many of us don't take the time to stop and rest. Sit in silence, allowing your thoughts to go wherever they go, and enjoy some peace for a full hour. You may be surprised at what you feel when you allow yourself to listen.

43. EXPLORE YOUR RELATIONSHIP WITH A HIGHER POWER ❑

Whether it's one you're familiar with or you make an effort to understand more about other beliefs, choose one or more religions or spiritual practices to learn more about. Research on the internet, attend a church or temple service, or, with an open mind and heart, discuss faith of different varieties with loved ones. Below, write the actions you will take to expand your relationship with a higher power.

44. PRACTICE AFFIRMATIONS ❏

What is one thing you would like to bring into your life? Spend a week telling yourself, either out loud or silently, that you have it and appreciate it. As our bodies and minds are connected, the more you believe in something the more you will bring it into your life. Some common affirmations for retirees include, "I'm glad to be able to spend more time with my hobbies," "My health remains excellent all through retirement," and "Having time to do whatever I want is very freeing." Write some affirmations that speak to you here:

❏ _____

❏ _____

❏ _____

❏ _____

❏ _____

❏ _____

❏ _____

❏ _____

❏ _____

❏ _____

❏ _____

❏ _____

❏ _____

❏ _____

❏ _____

CHAPTER 8
CREATING PURPOSE

You likely found purpose in your life through your job, from progressing in your career, and in your family, from raising your kids into healthy, productive adults. Now that you don't have a job to attend each day and your kids are all grown up, maybe even with families of their own, you might feel at a loss and rather purposeless in retirement. This free-floating feeling and lack of commitments, projects, or accountability can quickly take a toll on your mood and mental health. Though watching as much TV as you want, traveling as often, as far, and as long as you want, and spending summers on the water and winters in the snow can look like heaven from afar and feel liberating and relaxing to begin with, after a while this leisure-filled existence can begin to feel meaningless. You will want to have purpose again, be a part of your community, and contribute. There are many ways you can do that.

45. VOLUNTEER YOUR TIME AND SKILLS ❑

Thinking about your skills, interests, and desire to help, what causes could you contribute to and make a difference for?

❑ _____

❑ _____

❑ _____

❑ _____

❑ _____

❑ _____

❑ _____

❑ _____

❑ _____

❑ _____

❑ _____

❑ _____

❑ _____

❑ _____

❑ _____

❑ _____

❑ _____

❑ _____

46. HELP LOVED ONES ❑

Many tasks we do are simple to us but monumental to someone else. Ask your loved ones if there is anything you can assist them with to help ease their burden.

Write down who you helped and what you did here.

❑ _____

❑ _____

❑ _____

❑ _____

❑ _____

❑ _____

❑ _____

❑ _____

❑ _____

❑ _____

❑ _____

❑ _____

❑ _____

❑ _____

❑ _____

❑ _____

❑ _____

47. DO A GOOD DEED. HELP A STRANGER AND EXPECT NOTHING IN RETURN ❏

Pay for a customer behind you, or, alternatively, if you see someone struggling to pay their own way, pay for them and expect nothing in return. Write the good deeds you performed here.

❏ _____

❏ _____

❏ _____

❏ _____

❏ _____

❏ _____

❏ _____

❏ _____

❏ _____

❏ _____

❏ _____

❏ _____

❏ _____

❏ _____

❏ _____

❏ _____

❏ _____

48. SPEND AN HOUR REFLECTING ON YOUR LIFE AND THE DIFFERENCE YOU HAVE MADE IN THE LIVES OF OTHERS ❑

Whether it be through achievements in work; helping strangers get back on their feet through charity; being an empathetic ear to others, or through raising confident and capable children, sometimes we lose track of the unique difference we have made in the world and the lives of others.

List your proudest moments of how you have made a difference here.

❑ _____

❑ _____

❑ _____

❑ _____

❑ _____

❑ _____

❑ _____

❑ _____

❑ _____

❑ _____

❑ _____

❑ _____

❑ _____

❑ _____

❑ _____

CHAPTER 9

LAUGH LIKE YOU MEAN IT

We all know it feels good to laugh, but sometimes there just doesn't seem to be anything worth laughing about. According to the study, "The Effect of Humor on Short-Term Memory in Older Adults: A New Component for Whole-Person Wellness,"[4] laughter can boost short-term memory and have other great effects on aging brains.

Laughter yoga, where groups make silly movements together and create simulated laughter until it becomes real belly laughs, sounds odd, but studies have shown that it can actually be really good for your health, from lowering stress levels to increasing brain function to providing aerobic exercise.

If there's nothing to laugh about, go out and make something to laugh about! It's good for your health and makes everyone around you feel good as well.

---

4   Gurinder Singh Bains, Lee S Berk, Noha S. Daher et al. "The Effect of Humor on Short-Term Memory in Older Adults: A New Component for Whole-Person Wellness." *Advances in Mind-Body Medicine* 28, no. 2 (2014): 16-24.

49. ATTEND A LAUGHTER YOGA CLASS ❑

THE ULTIMATE **RETIREMENT** BUCKET LIST

50. GO TO A STAND-UP COMEDY SHOW ❏

Who would you like to see that will be performing near you? Book your tickets and write here who you'll see and when.

Comedian:_____

Date and Time: _____ Venue: _____

Comedian:_____

Date and Time: _____ Venue: _____

Comedian:_____

Date and Time: _____ Venue: _____

Comedian:_____

Date and Time: _____ Venue: _____

Comedian:_____

Date and Time: _____ Venue: _____

Comedian:_____

Date and Time: _____ Venue: _____

Comedian:_____

Date and Time: _____ Venue: _____

Comedian:_____

Date and Time: _____ Venue: _____

51. WATCH BLOOPER REELS FOR YOUR FAVORITE MOVIES AND TV SHOWS ON YOUTUBE

Do more of what makes you laugh. Be it slapstick, stand-up comedy, animal antics, or something else, list what makes you laugh here and make a plan to experience more of it. Write what makes you laugh below.

What makes me laugh...

_____

_____

...and what I'll do to enjoy it more often.

_____

_____

———•—•———

What makes me laugh...

_____

_____

...and what I'll do to enjoy it more often.

_____

_____

———•—•———

What makes me laugh...

_____

_____

...and what I'll do to enjoy it more often.

_____

_____

———•—•———

What makes me laugh...

_____

_____

...and what I'll do to enjoy it more often.

_____

_____

———•—•———

What makes me laugh...

_____

_____

...and what I'll do to enjoy it more often.

_____

_____

52. PRANK LOVED ONES ❑

Depending on your personality, your friends and loved ones may never see this coming! Retirement doesn't mean you need to be a serious adult. Those days are over, you can be as free-spirited and creative as you choose. Giving someone a surprise or playing a tame joke on them can spike adrenaline and endorphins and make you both laugh. Shake up your relationships by surprising loved ones with some lighthearted silliness. But be sure to keep it lighthearted. It's no fun to receive devastating news only to be told it's a joke, or to be sprayed with water or covered in glitter in public or when running out the door.

Please note: Be mindful not to prank strangers or give a fright to anyone with anxiety, heightened stress, or a heart condition. Tailor your prank to those who will appreciate it.

❑ _____

❑ _____

❑ _____

❑ _____

❑ _____

❑ _____

❑ _____

❑ _____

❑ _____

❑ _____

❑ _____

❑ _____

53. PRACTICE SLEIGHT OF HAND TRICKS ❑

Research some magic tricks online to make the people in your life wonder where you were keeping these tricks all along!

List some magic tricks to learn and amaze others with here:

❑ _____

❑ _____

❑ _____

❑ _____

❑ _____

❑ _____

❑ _____

❑ _____

❑ _____

❑ _____

❑ _____

❑ _____

❑ _____

❑ _____

❑ _____

❑ _____

❑ _____

CHAPTER 10
CREATIVITY AND HOBBIES

In the past, you may have felt that hobbies and creative activities were indulgences you didn't have time for. Now is the perfect time to try all the things! Give it a go, stop what you don't enjoy, and persevere with those you do. Your life will be richer for it.

54. HOBBIES YOU HAVE ALWAYS WANTED TO TRY ❑

It doesn't matter if you continue it or not, finding out whether you enjoy it is the point. Pursue it if you do! List activities you'd like to try here. If there is anyone who might like to do one with you, add their name.

❑ _____

❑ _____

❑ _____

❑ _____

❑ _____

❑ _____

❑ _____

❑ _____

❑ _____

❑ _____

❑ _____

❑ _____

❑ _____

❑ _____

❑ _____

❑ _____

❑ _____

55. HOBBIES YOU ENJOYED IN THE PAST

Now is a great time to relearn and restart activities you always enjoyed. Choose the top three and write them here:

1. _____

2. _____

3. _____

56. NAME A STAR ❏

Leave a lasting legacy that is out of this world by naming a star after yourself or someone important to you through one of the many star registries that can be found online. While you're at it, invest in a telescope and learn your constellations and heavenly bodies.

57. TAKE A POTTERY CLASS ❏

Create a piece of art, decorative bowl, vase, or anything you can think of, and display your work in your home.

58. GO TO A PAINTING AND WINE CLASS ❏

With a bucket list buddy, go along for a new experience and enjoy creating, wine, and socializing with other casual artists.

59. WRITE A SHORT STORY, POEM, NOVEL, SONG, OR PLAY ❏

Write something that interests you, from your heart. It doesn't matter if it's good or bad and you don't need to show anyone. Just experience creating something that existed nowhere but inside you.

60. BUILD A SCULPTURE ❑

Be it abstract art made from bits and bobs around the house or a sculpture representing something you love, get started now!

61. JOIN A LOCAL THEATER GROUP ❑

Do you want to build sets? Do you love shopping and sourcing props? Would putting together costumes be a fun time for you? Do you play an instrument that would be great in the live band or orchestra for a musical? Are you ready to shine on stage, front and center?

62. BEGIN A DAILY BRAIN-TRAINING AND LOGIC-PUZZLE HABIT ❏

When they say, "use it or lose it," they're not just talking about your body but your brain. Exercise this all-important muscle and keep your mental skills sharp through brain-training quizzes, sudoku, and other logic puzzles, crosswords, word searches, and more. Increase the challenge by working in pen!

63. LEARN HOW TO DRAW YOUR FAVORITE ANIMAL ❏

CHAPTER 11
EDUCATION

What would you like to know more about this world and beyond? Pursue that knowledge through self-directed study, practicing a new skill, from calligraphy to fixing cars, or even enrolling in a short course and gaining a certificate or degree.

Not only is continual learning a fascinating pastime, it's also an essential way to keep your mind active and brain performance in peak condition. Intellectual engagement has been clinically proven to be significantly associated with brain performance in later life. Thankfully, there are plenty of ways to learn, from the library and documentary-specific TV stations to websites, and educational video courses. The world is your oyster. Delve deep into whatever intrigues you. Whether you study passively at your own leisure or get serious and decide to enroll in an accredited course is up to you. You can learn a new language on an app, develop a craft through a practical kit available for purchase in a big-box store, or study an astounding breadth of topics from experts on YouTube.

64. TOPICS TO LEARN MORE ABOUT ❏

Why does the Earth revolve around the sun? How are diamonds made? What exactly was the Tunguska event? What was the Spanish Inquisition about? List 15 things you've always wondered about here.

❏ 1. _____

❏ 2. _____

❏ 3. _____

❏ 4. _____

❏ 5. _____

❏ 6. _____

❏ 7. _____

❏ 8. _____

❏ 9. _____

❏ 10. _____

❏ 11. _____

❏ 12. _____

❏ 13. _____

❏ 14. _____

❏ 15. _____

65. GO DOWN A WIKIPEDIA RABBIT HOLE ❏

You may go down a rabbit hole on the internet when you visit a website (such as Wikipedia, Reddit, or YouTube) to find more information about a specific topic, then follow links to explore more and more obscure topics that seem interesting to you. There is no right or wrong way to traverse the rabbit hole! Follow the links that look interesting to you!

66. LEARN ANOTHER LANGUAGE ❏

Use a language app like Duo Lingo, borrow a language book or CD from your local library, or buy one from your local bookstore.

67. DO IT YOURSELF ❑

Are there any repairs you need to get done around the house that you never felt handy enough to do yourself? Give it a go! Paint that room, install that floating shelf, watch some tutorials and replace the carpet yourself. What do you have to lose? You can save money by making repairs around your home (but let's be safe about it, maybe leave electrical wiring to an electrician). And even if all doesn't go according to plan, you will learn a lot of new skills and can always hire someone to help you finish the job (including what not to do). List some project ideas to get started on below:

❑ _____

❑ _____

❑ _____

❑ _____

❑ _____

❑ _____

❑ _____

❑ _____

❑ _____

❑ _____

❑ _____

❑ _____

❑ _____

❑ _____

❑ _____

68. BUILD SOMETHING WITH YOUR HANDS

❏

Be it something small like jewelry, big like a table, or complicated like a computer, making it yourself will give it extra meaning, increase your confidence, and help you gain a fun new skill!

❏ _____

❏ _____

❏ _____

❏ _____

❏ _____

❏ _____

❏ _____

❏ _____

❏ _____

❏ _____

❏ _____

❏ _____

❏ _____

❏ _____

❏ _____

❏ _____

❏ _____

CHAPTER 12
LIVING DANGEROUSLY

Throughout your childhood, there were likely a lot of things you wanted to do and experience that your parents wouldn't allow. Some of those limitations may have stuck with you throughout your life if you internalized your parents' worries, anxieties, rules, or boundaries.

When you were a child, your parents were responsible for your well-being. They loved you and wanted you to be safe. Or maybe they didn't want you to make a mess. You might have been forbidden from jumping in mud puddles or having food fights because your parents simply didn't want to have to clean up after you.

But you're not a child anymore! You know what you're capable of and how far you can push yourself outside your comfort zone. You're not going to have a food fight at your parents' house. If you're lucky enough that they're still around, you'd never ask them to clean up after you. So what's stopping you from doing those exciting, daring, or unusual activities you've waited your whole life to do? If your health allows, do all the things! Here are some ideas to get you started.

69. TAKE THE CHILI PEPPER OR HOT AND SPICY NOODLE CHALLENGE ❏

Keep the milk and antacids close and take the challenge with friends or family. Whoever eats the most peppers, or the hottest pepper, wins!

Challenge food:_____

Amount eaten:_____

Participants:_____

Winner:_____ Date:_____

Challenge food:_____

Amount eaten:_____

Participants:_____

Winner:_____ Date:_____

Challenge food:_____

Amount eaten:_____

Participants:_____

Winner:_____ Date:_____

Challenge food:_____

Amount eaten:_____

Participants:_____

Winner:_____ Date:_____

70. DRIVE A RACE CAR ❏

Sign up for a race car driving experience at a racing track near you, or include this exhilarating activity on a day trip or weekend away.

71. GO WHITE WATER RAFTING, ZIPLINING, OR SWIMMING WITH SHARKS ❏

Enjoy an adrenaline rush!

72. DYE YOUR HAIR A WILD COLOR OR CUT YOUR OWN HAIR ❑

While this sounds scary, ultimately your hair will grow back anyway, so what does it matter if your experiment doesn't come out as expected?

73. DRESS LIKE THE OPPOSITE SEX ❑

You don't need to leave the house to try on some clothes you'd never wear. See what it feels like in (literally) someone else's shoes.

74. GO TO AN EVENT YOU WOULDN'T TYPICALLY CHOOSE ❑

Don't think the ballet is your thing? Can't understand the appeal of monster truck rallies? What's the point of a farmers market anyway? List an event or activity (or several!) you don't see the appeal of and give it a go. You might surprise yourself!

❑ _____

❑ _____

❑ _____

❑ _____

❑ _____

❑ _____

❑ _____

❑ _____

❑ _____

❑ _____

❑ _____

❑ _____

❑ _____

❑ _____

❑ _____

❑ _____

CHAPTER 13

BIG DARING DREAMS

Do something that scares you. That thing you just thought of? That's the thing. As long as you can be safe when doing it, try it. Stretch yourself outside your comfort zone. If not now, when?

75. START A PART-TIME BUSINESS USING THE SKILLS YOU'VE DEVELOPED OVER YOUR LIFETIME ❑

With the loss of income during retirement, a bit of extra cash can be a good incentive to start a business. Without the stress of having to support yourself from it, you can get creative and make it something you're passionate about through skills you're already good at. Will you sell knitted items on Etsy? Are you a great gardener who could tend to your neighbors' gardens ? How about designing art to print on demand and sell online ? Do you love to write? Consider writing books or articles for publication. Think outside the box about your skills and passions, and list some ideas here:

_____

_____

_____

_____

_____

_____

_____

_____

_____

_____

_____

_____

76. TRAIN FOR AND COMPETE IN A MARATHON ❏

Training for a marathon takes a lot of commitment, mental endurance, and physical endurance, not just on the big day but in the months and weeks leading up to it. Prove to yourself you can do anything you set your mind to.

77. PERFORM LIVE ❏

Singing, slam poetry, stand-up comedy—if you've held a secret dream of being in the spotlight on a stage, big or small, take that leap.

78. ENTER THAT COMPETITION ❏

If you have a hobby, be it art, dancing, writing, crochet, photography, woodworking, cooking, a team sport, whatever it may be, but you have never had the confidence to enter competitions, now is the time to step up to the plate, be confident in your passion, and show the world what you're made of.

CHAPTER 14
SEASONAL BUCKET LISTS

As the months go by, the weather changes and the days get hotter or colder. Here, you'll find activities to take up at specific times of the year when the season makes them most enjoyable. Embrace the playfulness and silly side that remains from your youth by visiting water parks and starting snowball fights. Embark on adventures you loved before or brand-new adventures to enjoy for the first time. The following suggestions for all four seasons will help you make the most of your time all year round.

SUMMER

79. VISIT A WATER PARK ❏

With adult friends or with the grandkids, don't just sit on the sidelines but get wet on the slides!

80. CONQUER A FEAR OF HEIGHTS AND DIVE/JUMP OFF THE HIGH DIVING BOARD ❏

81. GO TO AN OUTDOOR CINEMA ❏

Pack a blanket, warm clothes, and a camp chair. The day might have been warm but even summer evenings can get a little chilly. Enjoy the natural surroundings, a balmy breeze, and a fun summertime flick outdoors.

82. GO JET BOATING ❏

Enjoy an adrenaline rush as you zoom past other boats and whip around on the water doing 360° spins. Make sure you hold on tight!

83. GO CAMPING/GLAMPING ❏

If the days of camping out in nature where the only restroom is a secluded bush are behind you, then go ahead and pitch that tent in the backyard, roast some marshmallows, and tell scary stories to the grandkids over the fire, be it a real one or a video playing on the iPad. Fill the tent with cushions and comfort for a fun night under the stars. If those cushions don't cut it, simply sneak back to bed! This is your camping adventure, so do it however it makes you happy. List a few spots you'd like to go below:

❏ _____

❏ _____

❏ _____

❏ _____

❏ _____

❏ _____

❏ _____

❏ _____

❏ _____

❏ _____

❏ _____

❏ _____

❏ _____

❏ _____

❏ _____

AUTUMN

84. JUMP IN THE FALLEN LEAVES ❑

Before bagging up all the leaves for disposal, jump into the pile and feel like a kid again.

85. CARVE A JACK-O'-LANTERN ❑

Whether your design is scary or silly, grab some loved ones and make an afternoon of it.

86. DRESS UP FOR HALLOWEEN, OR DRESS UP YOUR HOUSE FOR HALLOWEEN ❑

When was the last time you went all out for Halloween, gave candy to children at your door, or offered to take the children of a loved one trick-or-treating to allow their parents a night to themselves? Get out there and enjoy being a part of the neighborhood (and getting to know some neighbors you don't know!) as the streets bustle with families enjoying each other's company on this spookiest of nights!

87. HOST A FRIENDS-GIVING PARTY ❑

It doesn't have to be an elaborate event. Invite loved ones whom you don't traditionally see during the holiday party season to an afternoon or evening at home or out to celebrate what they mean to you.

88. HAVE A FOOD FIGHT

Pick some ooey, gooey foods, some flours, sauces, and liquids, grab your bucket list buddies, and battle it out. Let's get messy!

89. JUMP IN THE MUD

Make sure you have a nearby hose to clean yourself off before going inside again!

WINTER

Either enjoy the crisp winter air and snowfall at home or take a trip somewhere snowy to enjoy the novelty of soft snowflakes, iced-over ponds, and snow crunching underfoot.

90. HAVE A SNOWBALL FIGHT ❑

If you live in snowy climates, heavy snowfall can make for a lot of work around your home. If you find snow to be a burden, change up your mindset by adding some fun and unexpected silliness to your day: Challenge someone (or many someones!) to a snowball fight.

91. MAKE A SNOWMAN ❑

How long has it been since you built a person out of freshly fallen snow? Take a cool and crisp trip down memory lane with a new friend made of snow.

92. MAKE A SNOW ANGEL ❏

Put on your waterproof gear, flop into the snow, and gaze up at the sky to see the world from a different angle as you flap your arms and legs beside you. How does your angel compare now with what it looked like when you did it as a child?

93. INVITE LOVED ONES OVER TO BAKE AND DECORATE CHRISTMAS COOKIES ❏

Surprise them all at the end of a successful (or unsuccessful) baking session with mulled wine or egg nog you prepared yourself! Then, as the sun goes down, snuggle up in comfy clothes in front of a fire with a dog or cat nearby, and share life stories and delicious fresh-baked cookies.

94. HAVE AN AT-HOME SPA DAY ❏

With the weather miserable outside, spend it warm and snug at home pampering yourself. Buy some face masks or mix together your own, paint your nails, sit back, take deep, relaxing breaths, sip on some champagne, and luxuriate in the moment.

95. HAVE A CHRISTMAS
MOVIE MARATHON ❏

Snuggle up under a blanket, enjoy the sickly sweetness of bad holiday movies, and spend a day or night getting into the Christmas spirit.

96. HOST A TACKY CHRISTMAS SWEATER PARTY

Create a new annual holiday tradition with party games and a worst-sweater winner, invite loved ones, acquaintances you'd like to know better, and friends who may not have met each other. If you like all these people, then chances are they might like each other as well!

SPRING

97. WALK IN A PARK AND LITERALLY STOP TO SMELL THE FLOWERS ❏

Take your time to actually look at the flowers and leaves and intricacies of nature. Watch butterflies and bees pollinating flowers. Notice all the life going on around you.

98. PERFORM A BACKYARD PLAY WITH THE CHILDREN IN YOUR LIFE ❏

Write it yourself or with the kids, or perform your own rendition of a favorite story. Dress up, choreograph some silly moves, set up chairs outside, and let the show begin!

99. GET UP EARLY, LISTEN TO THE BIRDS, WATCH THE SUN RISE, AND WONDER AT THE BEAUTY OF NATURE ☐

100. REVISIT THE PLAYFULNESS OF YOUR CHILDHOOD AND HAVE A RACE ROLLING DOWN A GRASSY HILL ☐

101. TRY OUT NEW CUISINES AT AN INTERNATIONAL FOOD FESTIVAL ❏

Wander the stalls and inhale the aromas, enjoy the atmosphere, and maybe even discover your new favorite food to cook at home.

Festival: _____

Cuisine: _____

Favorite dish: _____

Festival: _____

Cuisine: _____

Favorite dish: _____

Festival: _____

Cuisine: _____

Favorite dish: _____

Festival: _____

Cuisine: _____

Favorite dish: _____

Festival: _____

Cuisine: _____

Favorite dish: _____

Festival: _____

Cuisine: _____

Favorite dish: _____

CONCLUSION

There you have it! A bucket list of 101 ideas—and hundreds more of your own—for a healthy and strong, adventurous, mind-expanding, fulfilling, playful, meditative, and meaningful retirement to help you expand your comfort zone so you can focus on and live the life you truly desire for the decades to come.

Your retirement years are going to be your best ones yet.

THE ULTIMATE **RETIREMENT** BUCKET LIST

APPENDIX

Here you'll find worksheets to help you take action toward your goals and build strong habits to make it the best, healthiest and most rewarding retirement it could be.

Photocopy the pages here and use them again and again to track your progress in prioritizing what is important to you.

WEEKLY MEDICATION TRACKER

Month: _____

MEDICATION	DOSAGE	MON	TUES	WED	THUR	FRI	SAT	SUN

WEEKLY MEDICATION TRACKER

Month: _____

MEDICATION	DOSAGE	MON	TUES	WED	THUR	FRI	SAT	SUN

WEEKLY MEDICATION TRACKER

Month: _____

MEDICATION	DOSAGE	MON	TUES	WED	THUR	FRI	SAT	SUN

WEEKLY MEDICATION TRACKER

Month: _____

MEDICATION	DOSAGE	MON	TUES	WED	THUR	FRI	SAT	SUN

HABIT TRACKER

Month: _____

HABIT	1	2	3	4	5	6	7	8	9	10	11	12	13	14	15	16	17	18	19	20	21	22	23	24	25	26	27	28	29	30	31

HABIT TRACKER

Month: _____

HABIT	1	2	3	4	5	6	7	8	9	10	11	12	13	14	15	16	17	18	19	20	21	22	23	24	25	26	27	28	29	30	31

HABIT TRACKER

Month: _____

HABIT	1	2	3	4	5	6	7	8	9	10	11	12	13	14	15	16	17	18	19	20	21	22	23	24	25	26	27	28	29	30	31

HABIT TRACKER

Month: _____

HABIT	1	2	3	4	5	6	7	8	9	10	11	12	13	14	15	16	17	18	19	20	21	22	23	24	25	26	27	28	29	30	31

SMART GOAL-SETTING WORKSHEET

Goal: _____

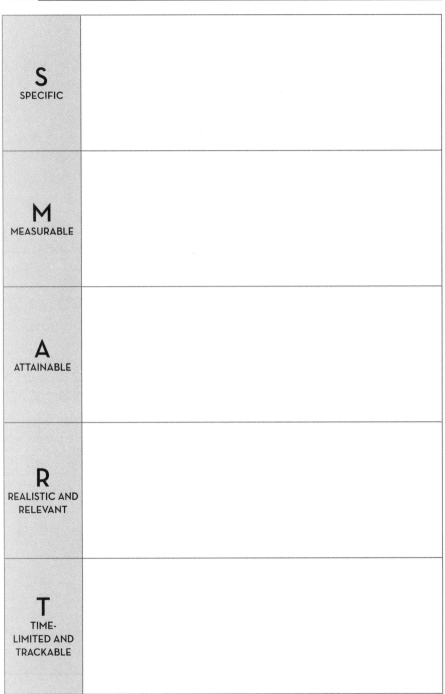

S SPECIFIC	
M MEASURABLE	
A ATTAINABLE	
R REALISTIC AND RELEVANT	
T TIME-LIMITED AND TRACKABLE	

SMART GOAL-SETTING WORKSHEET

Goal: _____

S SPECIFIC	
M MEASURABLE	
A ATTAINABLE	
R REALISTIC AND RELEVANT	
T TIME-LIMITED AND TRACKABLE	

SMART GOAL-SETTING WORKSHEET

Goal: _____

S SPECIFIC	
M MEASURABLE	
A ATTAINABLE	
R REALISTIC AND RELEVANT	
T TIME- LIMITED AND TRACKABLE	

ACKNOWLEDGMENTS

I would like to thank Claire Sielaff at Ulysses Press for seeing something special in my vision to help users live their retirement years in a way that is right for them, on their terms, with no regrets. Thanks also to editor Ashten Evans for guiding me through publication with Ulysses and encouraging my thoughts and feedback throughout the process, and Renee Rutledge for enhancing my language and making the best bucket list for the reader we can.

Thanks to my friend, writing cheerleader, and earliest reader, Chaille Bos, for her comments during my revisions, and to my family for always supporting my endeavors to live a life retired Sarah will be proud of.

ABOUT THE AUTHOR

Sarah Billington is the owner of boutique lifestyle brand Edwina Ray, offering gorgeous homewares and stationery, including coloring books and themed notebooks plus guided journals for cultivating gratitude, health and wellness, planning a wedding, recording travel adventures, achieving goals, and more. She is also a fiction author and, when not crafting stories, interesting homewares, or stationery to help you plan your life, she can be found at home with good friends and her cats.